# PRO FOOTBALL'S
# STARS OF THE OFFENSE

## by Michael Sandler

Consultant: Norries Wilson
Head Football Coach
Columbia University

BEARPORT
PUBLISHING
New York, New York

**Credits**
Cover and Title Page, © Stephen Dunn/Getty Images and © AP Images/Marcio Jose Sanchez and © AP Images/Darron Cummings; TOC-L, © Tom Dahlin/Getty Images; TOC-R, © Dilip Vishwanat/Getty Images; 4, © Carlos Gonzalez/Minneapolis Star Tribune/MCT/Newscom; 5L, © AiWire/Newscom; 5R, © Nick Laham/Getty Images; 6, © NFL Photos/Getty Images; 7, © Scott Boehm/Getty Images; 8, © NFL Photos/Getty Images; 9, © Dilip Vishwanat/Getty Images; 10, © NFL Photos/Getty Images; 11, © Tom Dahlin/Getty Images; 12, © NFL Photos/Getty Images; 13, © Joe Robbins/Getty Images; 14, © NFL Photos/Getty Images; 15, © Al Bello/Getty Images; 16, © NFL Photos/Getty Images; 17, © Chris Lee/St. Louis Post-Dispatch/MCT/Newscom; 18, © NFL Photos/Getty Images; 19, © AP Images/Paul Jasienski; 20, © NFL Photos/Getty Images; 21, © AP Images/Paul Spinelli; 22L, © Tom Dahlin/Getty Images; 22R, © Dilip Vishwanat/Getty Images.

Publisher: Kenn Goin
Senior Editor: Lisa Wiseman
Creative Director: Spencer Brinker
Design: Keith Plechaty
Photo Researcher: Picture Perfect Professionals, LLC

*Library of Congress Cataloging-in-Publication Data*

Sandler, Michael, 1965–
   Pro football's stars of the offense / by Michael Sandler ; consultant, Norries Wilson.
      p. cm. — (Football-o-rama)
   Includes bibliographical references and index.
   ISBN-13: 978-1-936088-26-3 (library binding)
   ISBN-10: 1-936088-26-6 (library binding)
   1. Football players—United States—Biography.
   2. Football—Offense. I. Wilson, Norries. II. Title.
   GV939.A1S2535 2011
   796.332092'2—dc22
   [B]
                         2010013001

For more information, write to Bearport Publishing Company, Inc., 101 Fifth Avenue, Suite 6R, New York, New York 10003. Printed in the United States of America in North Mankato, Minnesota.

062010
042110CGC

10 9 8 7 6 5 4 3 2 1

# CONTENTS

# STARS OF THE OFFENSE

In NFL **offenses**, the players who often receive the most attention are the quarterbacks. As leaders of their teams, they usually get the credit for wins or the blame for losses. Ten other players, however, take the field on each offensive play. Each one has a role in gaining yards and scoring points. Each one is important in helping his team win.

**Minnesota Vikings running back Adrian Peterson carries the ball downfield during a game against the Seattle Seahawks in 2009.**

This book features the talented athletes who play at the different offensive positions. You will learn about **running backs**, such as Chris Johnson, Adrian Peterson, and Le'Ron McClain, who carry the ball. You'll meet Andre Johnson, Larry Fitzgerald, and Dallas Clark, the **receivers** who catch the passes. You will also discover hard-working players on the **offensive line**, such as Ryan Clady and Nick Mangold, who contribute to every play. Each one is a star of the offense!

Arizona Cardinals wide receiver Larry Fitzgerald goes to make a catch in a game against the Green Bay Packers in January 2010.

New York Jets center Nick Mangold (#74) gets ready to snap the ball in a 2009 game against the New England Patriots.

# NICK MANGOLD #74
# NEW YORK JETS

**Position:** Center
**Born:** 1/13/1984 in Centerville, Ohio
**College:** Ohio State

**Pro Bowls:** 2
**Height:** 6' 4" (1.93 m)
**Weight:** 305 pounds (138 kg)

Offensive linemen form a wall with their huge bodies to give a quarterback time to throw and running backs space to move. With Nick Mangold at the center of this wall, **defenders** can't get over or around it. In 2009, Nick's work keeping defenders away helped the New York Jets lead the entire NFL in **rushing** with 172 yards (157 m) per game.

Equally important, Nick did a great job protecting **rookie** quarterback Mark Sanchez. With rookies, confidence is crucial. A young quarterback can get nervous if he feels he's not protected. With Nick right in front of him, Mark felt safe all season long. So safe that the Jets advanced to the **AFC Championship Game**.

## BIG GAME
### JANUARY 9, 2010

In the Jets' 24-14 playoff win against the Cincinnati Bengals, Nick held off the Bengals' **pass rushers** the entire game. This allowed Mark Sanchez to complete 12 of 15 passes without being **intercepted** or **sacked**.

Nick (#74) protects quarterback Mark Sanchez (#6) during the playoff game against the Cincinnati Bengals in 2010.

# RYAN CLADY #78
## DENVER BRONCOS

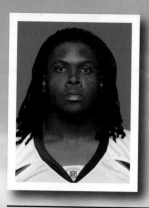

**Position:** Offensive Tackle
**Born:** 9/6/1986 in Long Beach, California
**College:** Boise State

**Pro Bowls:** 1
**Height:** 6' 6" (1.98 m)
**Weight:** 325 pounds (147 kg)

Along with centers, tackles and guards make up the wall that protects NFL passers. When offensive tackle Ryan Clady of the Denver Broncos is part of the wall, it might as well be made of steel. In his first 20 games as an NFL left tackle, he didn't allow a full sack once! That's an NFL record for players beginning their careers.

Trying to get past Ryan is like trying to tunnel through a mountain. At 325 pounds (147 kg), he's enormous. Despite his size, however, he's unbelievably quick on his feet. His long arms and strong hands keep even the mightiest pass rushers off balance.

## BIG GAME
### DECEMBER 7, 2008

During the Broncos' 24-17 win over the Kansas City Chiefs, Ryan was able to hold back the Chiefs' pass rushers play after play. As a result, Broncos quarterback Jay Cutler had plenty of time to find open receivers. After the game, Ryan was voted NFL Rookie of the Week.

Ryan blocks during the game against the Kansas City Chiefs in 2008.

# ADRIAN PETERSON #28
## MINNESOTA VIKINGS

**Position:** Running Back
**Born:** 3/21/1985 in Palestine, Texas
**College:** Oklahoma

**Pro Bowls:** 3
**Height:** 6' 1" (1.85 m)
**Weight:** 217 pounds (98 kg)

In 2007, in just his eighth NFL game, running back Adrian Peterson ran for 296 yards (271 m), an all-time NFL record. Then in his second season, Adrian led the entire league in rushing, piling up 1,760 yards (1,609 m).

In 2009, Adrian showed his **versatility**. The Vikings picked up the great Brett Favre at quarterback. Not surprisingly, the coaches decided to have the team pass more to take advantage of Brett's amazing throwing skills. With fewer chances to rush the ball, Adrian displayed his ability to catch. He ended up with 43 **receptions**, and led the league with 18 rushing touchdowns. Most important, the Vikings advanced all the way to the **NFC Championship Game**.

## BIG GAME
### November 4, 2007

During this game against the San Diego Chargers, Adrian set the single-game NFL rushing record. His 296 yards (271 m) included three touchdown runs of 1, 46, and 64 yards (.9, 42, and 59 m). The Vikings won the game, 35-17.

Adrian carries the ball during the November 2007 game against the San Diego Chargers.

# CHRIS JOHNSON #28
## TENNESSEE TITANS

**Position:** Running Back
**Born:** 9/23/1985 in Orlando, Florida
**College:** East Carolina

**Pro Bowls:** 2
**Height:** 5' 11" (1.80 m)
**Weight:** 200 pounds (91 kg)

After just two NFL seasons, people were already calling running back Chris Johnson the fastest man in football. When Chris sees even the tiniest opening in the defense, he runs through it in a flash. In 2009, Chris set an NFL single-season record for **total yards from scrimmage**—2,509 (2,294 m). He also became the sixth player ever to rush for more than 2,000 yards (1,829 m) in a season. Equally as incredible, in each of the last 11 games of the 2009 season, he reached the 100-yard (91-m) mark!

What's it like trying to stop Chris Johnson? Imagine trying to catch a lightning bolt—it's impossible!

## BIG PLAY
### September 20, 2009

Just after halftime in this game against the Houston Texans, Chris took the ball at the nine-yard (8-m) line. Following his blocker, guard Eugene Amano, he ran past the defenders and raced all the way downfield for a 91-yard (83-m) touchdown.

Chris runs with the football in the September 2009 game against the Houston Texans.

# LE'RON MCCLAIN #33
## BALTIMORE RAVENS

**Position:** Fullback
**Born:** 12/27/1984 in Fort Wayne, Indiana
**College:** Alabama

**Pro Bowls:** 2
**Height:** 6' 0" (1.83 m)
**Weight:** 260 pounds (118 kg)

Being a **fullback** isn't a high-profile job. Although fullbacks sometimes run the ball, most of the time they block for other running backs. The ball carriers get the glory and the yards.

In 2008, Le'Ron McClain scored ten touchdowns as the Ravens' main ball carrier. Then in 2009, his role changed. He became lead blocker for the talented running back Ray Rice. Le'Ron didn't let this change bother him. Instead, he excelled in his new job. He cleared huge holes in the **defensive line** for Ray to run through, slamming into linemen like a wrecking ball.

Le'Ron is happy doing whatever the offense needs to win. He says, "Whenever my number is called in whatever way—blocking, running, or catching—I just continue to do whatever they want me to do."

## BIG GAME
### JANUARY 10, 2010

Le'Ron came up big in the Ravens' 33-14 playoff win over the New England Patriots. He made huge blocks for Willis McGahee and Ray Rice on touchdown runs. He also scored a touchdown of his own.

Le'Ron scores a touchdown in the January 10, 2010, game against the New England Patriots.

# ANDRE JOHNSON #80
## HOUSTON TEXANS

**Position:** Wide Receiver
**Born:** 7/11/1981 in Miami, Florida
**College:** Miami (Florida)

**Pro Bowls:** 4
**Height:** 6′ 3″ (1.91 m)
**Weight:** 225 pounds (102 kg)

Wide receiver Andre Johnson always had talent. His uncle Keith saw it right away when he first threw passes to four-year-old Andre. By high school, Andre's natural ability made him an **All-American**. Hard work, however, is what made him unstoppable.

In college, Andre saw older players working hard on their skills. "It rubbed off on me," he said. "I started going to the weight room. I started working on my **routes**."

The result of mixing talent and effort can be seen every time Andre races past an NFL **cornerback**. He led the NFL in **receiving yards** in 2008 and 2009, and has four career **Pro Bowl** selections. St. Louis Rams cornerback Ron Bartell says, "There's nobody that compares to him."

## BIG GAME
### DECEMBER 20, 2009

Andre made nine catches for 196 yards (179 m) in the Texans' 16-13 victory over the St. Louis Rams.

Andre catches a 49-yard (45-m) touchdown pass against the St. Louis Rams in 2009.

# LARRY FITZGERALD #11
## ARIZONA CARDINALS

**Position:** Wide Receiver
**Born:** 8/31/1983 in Minneapolis, Minnesota
**College:** Pittsburgh

**Pro Bowls:** 4
**Height:** 6' 3" (1.91 m)
**Weight:** 217 pounds (98 kg)

In high school, Larry Fitzgerald worked as a Minnesota Vikings ball boy. While he watched NFL receivers have incredible games, he thought: *I want to be like them*. Today, it's Larry that the ball boys dream about becoming. With great hands, perfect timing, and amazing leaping ability, he can catch high passes unlike any other receiver.

His best plays have come when it counts—in the playoffs. In the NFC Championship Game after the 2008 season, Larry made three first-half touchdown catches—an NFL record. Then in Super Bowl XLIII (43), Larry turned a short pass from quarterback Kurt Warner into a 64-yard (59-m) touchdown. Plays like these are what keep today's ball boys dreaming of the NFL.

## BIG GAME
### JANUARY 10, 2010

Larry caught two touchdown passes in the Cardinals' 51-45 playoff win over the Green Bay Packers. On his first, he cut to the middle, running between two defenders. After turning to catch the ball, he sprinted straight into the end zone for a 33-yard (30-m) touchdown. On the second, he made a diving grab for a Kurt Warner throw, resulting in an 11-yard (10-m) touchdown.

Larry reaches out to catch the football and score his second touchdown in the game against the Green Bay Packers in 2010.

# DALLAS CLARK #44
## INDIANAPOLIS COLTS

**Position:** Tight End
**Born:** 6/12/1979 in Livermore, Iowa
**College:** Iowa

**Pro Bowls:** 1
**Height:** 6' 3" (1.91 m)
**Weight:** 252 pounds (114 kg)

Like most **tight ends**, Dallas Clark does a little bit of everything, from blocking to catching passes. His specialty, however, is making some of the Indianapolis Colts' biggest plays.

A great example came in September 2009 against the Miami Dolphins. On the game's first play, Dallas used his speed to get open at midfield. He caught Peyton Manning's pass, broke a tackle, and ran all the way into the end zone for an 80-yard (73-m) touchdown.

Dallas went on to have his best ever NFL season. He was rewarded with his first Pro Bowl invitation. Sadly, Dallas couldn't make the game. He was too busy practicing for the Colts' appearance in Super Bowl XLIV (44)!

## BIG PLAY
### JANUARY 24, 2010

In the final quarter of this AFC Championship Game, Dallas Clark made a 15-yard (14-m) touchdown catch. The score gave the Colts a ten-point lead over the New York Jets. Indianapolis went on to win 30-17 and moved on to Super Bowl XLIV (44).

Dallas catches the ball during the game against the New York Jets in January 2010.

21

# THE OFFENSE

The offense is an important part of any football team. The players that make up the offense are responsible for scoring points. Here's a look at what they do as well as an example of how they line up on the field.

## END ZONE

### Wide Receiver
**main jobs:** run pass routes; get open to catch a quarterback's passes

### Offensive Linemen
**main jobs:** protect the quarterback on passing plays; create space for the ball carrier on rushing plays; the center begins each play by snapping the ball to the quarterback

Offensive Tackle — OT
Guard — G
Center — C
Guard — G
Offensive Tackle — OT

TE

### Wide Receiver
WR

WR

### Quarterback
**main jobs:** lead the offense by calling plays; pass the ball to receivers; hand the ball off to running backs

QB

### Tight End
**main jobs:** catch passes; block for running backs

FB

RB

### Fullback
**main job:** block and clear the way for the ball carrier

### Running Back
**main job:** carry the ball on rushing plays

# GLOSSARY

**AFC Championship Game** (AY-EFF-SEE CHAM-pee-uhn-*ship* GAME) a playoff game that decides which American Football Conference (AFC) team will go to the Super Bowl

**All-American** (*awl*-uh-MER-uh-kuhn) a high school or college athlete who is named one of the best at his position in the entire country

**cornerback** (KOR-nur-bak) a player on defense who has the job of covering the other team's receivers

**defenders** (di-FEN-durz) players who try to stop other players from scoring

**defensive line** (di-FENSS-iv LINE) the group of players (made up of defensive tackles and defensive ends) at the line of scrimmage who try to pressure the quarterback and tackle running backs

**fullback** (FUL-bak) a player whose job it is to block defenders, keeping them out of the way of running backs; this player may also run with the ball

**intercepted** (*in*-tur-SEP-tid) caught by a player on the other team

**NFC Championship Game** (EN-EFF-SEE CHAM-pee-uhn-*ship* GAME) a playoff game that decides which National Football Conference (NFC) team will go to the Super Bowl

**offenses** (AW-fenss-iz) the group of players on a team who are responsible for scoring points

**offensive line** (AW-fenss-iv LINE) the group of players (made up of tackles, guards, and a center) at the line of scrimmage who block for running backs and work to protect the quarterback

**pass rushers** (PASS RUHSH-urz) the group of defensive players who try to tackle the quarterback before he throws the ball

**Pro Bowl** (PROH BOHL) the NFL's all-star game for its very best players

**receivers** (ri-SEE-vurz) players who catch passes

**receiving yards** (ri-SEE-ving YARDZ) yards gained on a passing play

**receptions** (ri-SEP-shuhnz) passes that are caught

**rookie** (RUK-ee) a first-year player

**routes** (ROOTS) paths on the field that receivers travel along to be open to catching the ball on a play; these paths or routes are planned out ahead of the play

**running backs** (RUHN-ing BAKS) players who carry the ball on running plays

**rushing** (RUHSH-ing) running with the football

**sacked** (SAKT) when a quarterback gets tackled behind the line of scrimmage

**tight ends** (TITE ENDZ) offensive players who line up next to tackles, block for running backs, and catch passes as receivers

**total yards from scrimmage** (TOH-tuhl YARDZ FRUHM SKRIM-ij) the total yards gained from both receiving and rushing

**versatility** (*vur*-suh-TILL-uh-tee) the ability to do many different kinds of activities

# BIBLIOGRAPHY

*The New York Times*

*The Sporting News Magazine*

*Sports Illustrated*

ESPN.com

NFL.com

# READ MORE

**Doeden, Matt.** *The World's Greatest Football Players*. Mankato, MN: Capstone Press (2010).

**Gigliotti, Jim.** *Linemen (Game Day)*. Pleasantville, NY: Gareth Stevens (2009).

**Sandler, Michael.** *Adrian Peterson (Football Heroes Making a Difference)*. New York: Bearport (2010).

**Sandler, Michael.** *Larry Fitzgerald (Football Heroes Making a Difference)*. New York: Bearport (2010).

# LEARN MORE ONLINE

To learn more about the NFL's stars of the offense, visit
**www.bearportpublishing.com/FootballORama**

# INDEX